STILL
BITTER,
MORE
BAGGAGE

STILL BITTER, MORE BAGGAGE

GOING FOR THE BRONZE

Sloane Tanen

PHOTOGRAPHS
BY STEFAN
HAGEN

BLOOMSBURY

First published in
Great Britain 2005

Copyright © 2005
by SLOANE TANEN

The moral right of the author has been asserted

Bloomsbury Publishing Plc, 38 Soho Square, London
W1D 3HB

A CIP catalogue record for this book is available from the
British Library

ISBN 0 7475 8156 8
ISBN-13 9780747581567

1 3 5 7 9 10 8 6 4 2

Designed by MATTHEW LENNING

Printed in China by
SOUTH CHINA
PRINTING CO

All papers used by Bloomsbury Publishing are natural,
recyclable products made from wood grown in well-
managed forests. The manufacturing processes
conform to the environmental regulations of
the country of origin.

www.sloanetanen.com

for
NED TANEN

Why was Dr. Pinto putting Elizabeth on the spot when all of their problems were so clearly Elroy's fault? After all, hadn't Elroy shown up to meet her friends in a sweater vest and clogs? Wasn't that a personal assault?

Mrs. Bloom would have preferred the International House of Pancakes, but Hooters was nice too. The boys were certainly enjoying themselves, and wasn't that what Mother's Day was all about?

"I don't see a husband, children, or a career change in your future, but I do see two adorable kittens."

"And then, after her first day of solids, the consistency of her poop had really changed...
but it still had very little odour, which was so fascinating and..."

"Plié on cue, goddammit!!!" Big Momma hollered. "I didn't drag you clear across town to watch you drag your lazy ass across the stage!!!"

Reuben looked forward to his summers at Fat Camp Commando. Where else was his uncanny gift for sniffing out fig rolls so appreciated by his peers?

The President was about to learn just how unpopular his decision
was to pre-empt last Tuesday's *American Idol* with a televised press briefing.

It was the piercing sound of the dental drill that jolted Coco out of her beautiful dream.

*T*he *Young and the Restless* at 12:30,
The Bold and the Beautiful at 1:30, and *Passions* at 2:00.
Then, after a recap with her sister in Moscow,
Svetlana might fold the laundry.

Paige didn't care. She knew she had the right-of-way.

"I told you, I'm not hungry, Mother!"

Shari had a system: Udate on the laptop, Friends Reunited on the desktop, and Speeddate on the Palm. Her big and delicious husband was so close she could smell him.

"Disappointment. D-I-S-S-A-P-O-I-N-T-M-I-N-T. Disappointment."

Mr. Fontneau had a system for disciplining his less ambitious students.

One of Carrie's more serious problems was that her mother had failed to fill her in on the facts of life concerning "womanhood." So, when "it" finally happened, it was really quite terrifying.

Was it Mindy's imagination or was Roger whistling the theme song to *The Antiques Roadshow*?

Johnny was losing his patience. This bimbo had been droning on about the war for
six minutes now. It was prime-time Saturday night, for God's sake! "Let's hear about your Brazilian wax, honey."

It was Memorial Day weekend on Fire Island and one thing was clear: Cesar's success on Atkins was indisputable. He looked hot and *everyone* was noticing. Mitchell was frantic. Tonight he'd have to make the banana crumble and stop all this nonsense.

"I don't know, the last thing he said was something about being king of the world, and then I may have accidentally pushed him."

Every year Rabbi Lieberman broke his fast the same way.

Neil couldn't put his finger on it. Certainly they were very different, and yet...there was something so hauntingly familiar.

Maybe Celine did see Whitney leaving the bathroom with the toilet paper stuck to the bottom of her shoe...Was she her keeper?

Desperado. He couldn't let somebody love him. Now it's too late.

Beth rammed her fork into her thigh to squelch the tears of injustice from falling as Karen announced her engagement to Stewart. Yes, she would be Karen's bridesmaid, yes, she would buy her own blue taffeta dress, yes, she would throw Karen an engagement party, yes, she would plan the hen night, yes, yes, yes, yes, yes…

It occurred to Coco that calling 999 when she'd been sent to her room had probably not been the best idea.

Boris the boy genius was stumped.

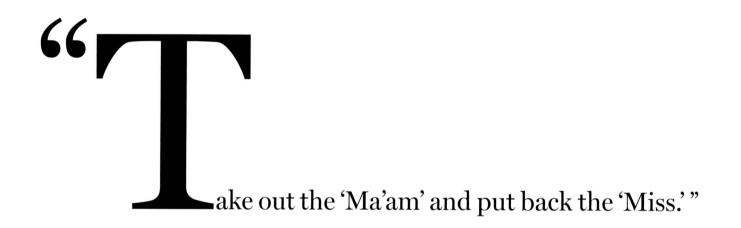

"Take out the 'Ma'am' and put back the 'Miss.'"

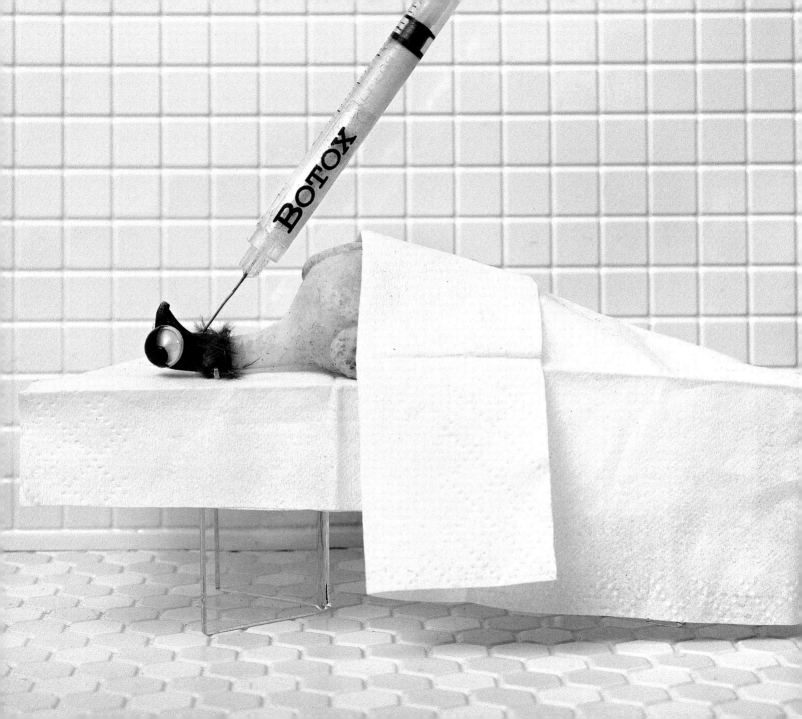

How many licks does it take to get to the centre of a chubby baby who's stolen all my glory? One, two...

After so many years of waiting, Charles was somewhat
sorry to find that up close Camilla smelled a bit of guacamole.

There was an old actress named Ruth
More than slightly obsessed with her youth
But no liposuction
Or deep reconstruction
Could soothe her like gin and vermouth

"I'm still Penny. Penny from the block!"

Carol had to ask herself: Was it more of a turnoff that Jack couldn't fix the leak, or that he refused to call the plumber...or was it a combo of the two that was suddenly making him so thoroughly revolting to her?

The day the tortoise and the hare got a lickin' from a chicken.

Nothing ever went Aaron's way. Bo Weinstein was spending his year abroad in Paris. Oliver Schwartz was in Florence. Aaron was eating walrus fat in an icebox. His mobile was frozen. Everybody smelled like herring.

Edgar spent every Monday night the same way. The missus was in kabbalah class and
would be sipping chai lattes with the girls until well into the evening. Ahhh, Monday nights!

All this exercise is working up quite an appetite, thought Bonnie as the angry mob chased her down the street. What should she eat tonight? Pork chop? Lamb chop? Mmmmm, veal chop!

Elisa had sauntered past the building site three times and nary a whistle could be heard.
She couldn't help but wonder, was she losing her game or just having an ugly day?

Howie was stoked. He had finally penetrated the inner circle and soon he would be Dungeon Master. Then wouldn't everybody from school be sorry.

The rescue effort for Joey Olsen would continue through the evening. But not for Mr. and Mrs. Olsen. They were tired. Maybe they'd just toss down the Game Boy and a flashlight and call it a night.

Mitchell and Cesar met at the "Gay Blades" two years ago. It was only natural that they should celebrate their anniversary skating. As the lights dimmed and "Gloria" began, Mitchell flew into a dazzling triple Lutz. Cesar's heart was bursting with pride. Never had a love been so true.

As Lourdes cradled the very last package, she had only one thought on her mind: This better be the red Birkin bag or else.

Tiffany was in no mood to hear her customer squabble about the £178.00 it would cost to correct her sallow complexion and wrinkly under-eye area. If she didn't want to pay for quality, she should high-tail her ass to T.K. Maxx and pick up some witch hazel and Lip Smacker.

"Karma IS a boomerang," thought Alistair as he sipped his lukewarm coffee and passed his change straight over the tip jar and right back into his pocket where it belonged.

"Oooohhh."

"Well, Barbara, I guess the best part of being an actress is that all of my insipid, pedestrian opinions on every subject from politics to motherhood are considered world news."

Coco dashed through the stop sign with her usual speed and agility. What would it be today?
A Popsicle, a Magnum...ahh, a Slush Puppie!

So far, twenty-three advisors had come to inform the king that he would indeed
have to go to the DVLA himself to renew his driver's licence.

It seemed to John Samuel that his wives got a little irritable around the twenty-second day of each month. But when the sole issue of *Heat* arrived on the twenty-third, things got downright scary.

Jonas was tired of his mother's penny-pinching. Last year it was five days of Hanukkah and one birthday gift. This year it was the handcrafted "scary ghost" costume. Oh, how he longed to be a Power Ranger…

Despite a rough morning, Virginia was still optimistic about the new school year.

Mitchell's mother was against the relationship from the start. It wasn't just that
her delicious potato latkes seemed to be the only thing Cesar wouldn't eat, but his tone was
very disrespectful every single time she asked him whether he was Jewish.

After all these years, Adelaide and Jeremiah still playfully bantered about whether they were indeed first or second cousins. But most felt the particulars didn't much matter.

"Oh, Lord, kumbaya."

Years ago Marion's shrink told her she needed to come up with a version of her childhood she could live with. She thought he said "aversion," and promptly took hold of a hideous tale of woe she particularly liked. It was thousands of pounds later that she finally sorted out the distinction.

Gladys and Harvey had waited until their golden years to see the Grand Canyon.
It was nice. But alas, she missed her cat and he missed his reclining armchair.

Saturday night was a blur, but Shelly knew one thing for certain.
This situation had the stink of too much booze and Big Huey written all over it.

ACKNOWLEDGMENTS

Once again, special thanks to both Stefan Hagen and Tracy James for their invaluable assistance. I'd also like to thank Colin Dickerman and the entire staff at Bloomsbury for all their support. Additional thanks to Amy Williams, Gary Taubes, Matthew Lenning, Holly Harrison, Kitty Hawks, Larry Lederman, Suzan Bymel, Gary Oshust, and the Tiny Doll House in Manhattan. Finally, particular gratitude to Randy Hague and his family at the Doll House Lady in San Marino, California.